PRAISE FOR JUDE AND

"This book explains websites so that they're not at all scary or boring; before I read it, I wouldn't have thought that was possible."

Dr Jennifer Jones – *Author of There's a Book in Every Expert*

"Their website creation process and hugely helpful planning resources all make for a creative and wonderfully managed experience which could otherwise be stressful or feel compromised."

Diana Theodores – *Presence & Performance Specialist*

"Chris and Jude have been amazing at bringing my vision for my website to life! They went above and beyond and were so supportive when I felt stuck with what to do. They took the pressure away and I am so excited to show off my website!"

Monique Basil-Wright – *Owner of The Wright Stationery*

"Chris and Jude have such a wide variety of expertise, it's not just technical, they really understand how to help you make your website work for you and stand out from the crowd."

Carly Campbell – *Nutrition and Wellness Specialist*

THE WEBSITE HANDBOOK
PLAN AND CREATE A WEBSITE THAT ATTRACTS
LEADS AND MAKES SALES

JUDE WHARTON

CHRIS WHARTON

2ND FLOOR DESIGNS LTD

Copyright © 2022 by Jude Wharton and Chris Wharton. All rights reserved.

No part of this book may be re-produced or used in any manner whatsoever without written permission except for brief quotations used in articles or reviews.

We have made every effort to credit all copyrighted materials used in this book. Any omissions will be rectified in future editions.

Editing: Jennifer Jones
Cover design: Chris Wharton

Printed in the United Kingdom
First printed 2022

ISBN: 978-1-7397067-0-8 (Paperback)
ISBN: 978-1-7397067-1-5 (eBook)

2nd Floor Designs Ltd
Southampton, Hampshire
SO52 9DY
weare2ndfloor.com

CONTENTS

1. INTRODUCTION	1
Our Background and Experience	1
The Importance of Having an Amazing Business Website	2
Examples of Website Success	4
What a Business Website Should Do	10
2. THE WEBSITE PLANNING PROCESS	15
The Importance of Planning Your Website	15
Your Ideal Client	16
The Purpose of Your Website	21
Doing Your Research	23
Creating Your Website Sitemap	29
Writing Your Content	34
Creating Wireframes (Page Layout)	41
Planning and Sourcing Your Images	43
The Importance of Brand Consistency	47
Creating Your Website Shopping List	48
3. CHOOSING YOUR PLATFORM AND SUPPORTING TECH	53
Website Platform Option Comparisons	54
Website Platform Prices	61
The Option of Getting It Done for You	62
Other Tech to Consider	64
4. WEB DESIGN HINTS AND TIPS	67
Why Good Design Matters	67
1. Give Things Room to Breathe	68
2. Visual Hierarchy	69
3. Images Are Everything	70
4. Getting Typography Right	71
5. Make Calls to Action Stand Out	74
6. Test, Test and Test Again	75

5. EVERYTHING AFTER YOUR WEBSITE IS LIVE: CONTENT, MAINTENANCE AND TRAFFIC — 78
The Importance of Adding New Content Regularly — 78
Regular Ongoing Content Planning — 80
How to Drive Traffic to Your Website (Using Analytics) — 87
Maintaining Your Website — 94

6. CONCLUSION — 96
How to Make Sure You Actually Do Everything We've Covered — 96
Final Thoughts — 97

Work with us — 99
About the Authors — 101
Acknowledgments — 103
Bibliography — 105

CHAPTER 1
INTRODUCTION

OUR BACKGROUND AND EXPERIENCE

We are excited!

Why are we so excited? Because we know how hard it is to create a website, with all the thinking, planning and procrastinating that goes along with it. This handbook is going to solve all of that for you!

We have helped literally thousands of small business owners and entrepreneurs create or improve their websites and online presence since we started our business in 2010 – through our little design agency, 2nd Floor Designs Ltd; our website and membership site template service, Ready Steady Websites®; or through being elite theme and plugin authors on Themeforest. Over the years, we have provided the designs, functionality and support that people have needed to make an impact online which has led to leads and sales, enabling them to grow their businesses.

That doesn't even take into consideration the work Chris did before we started our own business, managing and working on projects for some of the biggest names in motoring, finance, and business such as RBS, Renault, Coutts Bank,

IKEA, Mazda, Russell Investments, Kia, Citizens Bank, Adam & Company, WorldPay, Schroders, Tenneco, G4S, ABP, Olympus, Grant Thornton, Nexia and RAC.

Chris' knowledge combined with Jude's background in training and development have meant that we haven't just done the work for people, but we have also trained, supported, and enabled those small business owners and entrepreneurs to really understand their websites and their online presence so they can take control of them and continue to develop them as their businesses grow. This means they can push their online businesses to the next level. That's what we are going to do for you through this book.

If you use it fully, this book will give you knowledge and confidence, and it will become a valuable tool in helping you to create a website and online presence that showcases your business in the best possible way and generates leads, sales, and growth.

The book is a mixture of teaching, through stories and examples, and activities for you to get involved with and do. These are activities that we have used with **thousands** of people through Ready Steady Websites® that make a real difference to how successful their websites are.

So, let's get started and get your website and online presence in shape!

THE IMPORTANCE OF HAVING AN AMAZING BUSINESS WEBSITE

We truly believe that every business who deals directly with their consumer should value their online presence. There are so many ways that people refer to business websites – your online salesperson, your virtual shopfront, your virtual office, or the hub of your business.

However you think of it, if you had physical versions of all the things listed above you would value them and ensure they reflected well on your business.

Your salespeople would be kept up to date with changes in the business. They would have all the latest information about your products, services, and prices, and they would use language that's current and up to date when discussing these. You would also ensure they are well presented. Gone are the days of expecting everyone to wear a suit, but if they are meeting people face to face to discuss a potential sale, there would be certain standards you would expect them to meet. Why then do so many websites have incorrect details and prices and generally look a bit dated, tired, and scruffy?

If you had a shop window, you would refresh it every so often with a new display so that it catches a regular passer-by's eye. You would put signs about current deals they can get in the window to entice them inside and move new or popular products to the front of the window to attract people's attention and draw them in to see more. So why then do people not update their offers on their website, why do they not refresh the order of products regularly to reflect recent trends?

If you invited someone in for a meeting in your office, we hope you'd make a little bit of effort to make them welcome. You would ensure chairs are ready for them to sit down on, drinks are on offer and the workspace is uncluttered so you can concentrate on your meeting and the work you are going to be discussing. Perhaps you'd go one step further and have a dedicated meeting area away from the paperwork and hustle and bustle so that the meeting has a nice calm feel, making it easier to navigate. So why then are so many websites really cluttered, making it hard for the website visitor to find what they need and difficult for them to decide whether you provide what they want or not?

Fewer people now are shopping on the high street or visiting businesses in person, and if they are, they tend to do an online search first to see if it's worth making the trip. So, whether you have a fully online business or you have a physical premises with an online presence, it is really important that you place a lot of value on that online presence.

This is why we also recommend you have your own website and not just a social media presence. We chat to people who won't even consider buying from a business that doesn't have a website. They want to fully check out a business first before they explore working with them. They want to see that they value themselves by properly investing in their business, and they also want to see terms of service on the website and experiences of others so they know they are going down the right path.

These points are all worth considering if you are still at the stage where you are deciding whether a website is for you or you aren't sure whether updating your website is worth the time and effort. We can assure you it is. That time and effort will pay off when you see an increase in enquiries and sales coming through your website.

EXAMPLES OF WEBSITE SUCCESS

We are business owners ourselves. We started our business in 2010 and know how hard it can be to invest money in your business. We were lucky that between the two of us we had a lot of skills already covered and so didn't need to invest much money in other people's services in the early days. A couple of decent laptops and monitors and some computer software were our main expenses when we started. We didn't think twice about buying those. Without those we couldn't run a business, so there was no discussion about buying them. But as time goes on, you realise there are a lot of things you could spend money on that would probably help your business, but because you probably could try to do them yourself it's hard to see the benefit of getting a professional involved. It's especially hard when you feel there's no guarantee to the investment.

We know a lot of small business owners feel this way about their websites. They know they can create one by themselves for free on a number of website builders, and they think that will be absolutely fine. But we can tell you right now that spending time doing that is a complete waste of time when you could be spending that time doing what you do best in your business. You may feel like you've ticked the "have a business website box", but the website you've created will do nothing for your business and worse than that, may even put customers off.

Here are four examples of how doing a website right can make a huge difference and increase your business leads pretty much instantly.

The Construction Company Who Had a Dated Website Made by a Friend

A local construction company got in touch with us because they needed a new website. Someone had recommended us to them, and we had a chat with them on the phone, got a simple brief, and gave them an estimate on price. They thanked us and we didn't hear from them again for about two years.

This isn't uncommon. We know we aren't the cheapest web design company in our area and assumed they'd gone elsewhere, but then they phoned again. They hadn't gone elsewhere, they had just put it off, like so many business owners do. We'd felt their website looked dated and was letting them down when we first looked at it. It hadn't really changed over those two years, so it looked even worse. Web design and business websites had come on a long way in those two years, so in caparison with what else was on the web, the website really wasn't doing their business any favours.

Their website had been created by a friend and we hear

this story a lot … the friend has some time on their hands and so they take on the web project. Then they get busy or change career or you lose touch with them, and then you're left with a website that isn't being updated or maintained – also, you don't have full control over it and the friend can't help anymore. Then because you got the website for free the first time round you feel resentful for having to pay next time, which puts you in a bad mindset when it comes to investing in a website even though it's incredibly important for your business.

The second time they contacted us, they were prepared to put the time and money into getting their website properly sorted out. So much so that from their team of four, three came along to the meeting to scope the website out properly and kick off the project. In that meeting, we decided that they really needed to get their current website offline, so we created a quick holding page to go up in its place with their logo, business name, a brief statement about what they do, the locations they cover and a way to get in contact with them.

This holding page looked lovely, it was clean and simple and had an easy call to action for people to take. From that holding page they got more enquiries than they'd had from their terribly cluttered out of date website over the last few years. Yes, years!! More enquiries in a couple of months than they had in years.

This is a real life example of how bad a poor website can be for your business. If you know you are in that position and you're putting off getting a new website for fear of investing time and money, this shows that it will be worth it!

The Builder Who Was Fine with Word of Mouth Work

We aren't picking on the construction industry, honest! For the sake of balance, we have worked with a builder who was very on top of their online presence. This one, however, was not. He didn't have a website at all, despite his sister-in-law who was a marketing expert telling him over and over that he really should.

He didn't have much of an online presence and was happy with getting work through word of mouth, which kept his business ticking over alright, and that's OK but what if the word of mouth work dries up? After a while that is possible. If you aren't actively working to expand your network in some way, eventually you will exhaust it. Also, larger building projects aren't things that people tend to need doing over and over again, so repeat work isn't as likely as in some other areas of business. So, it really would be good for him to get himself out there online.

In the end he gave in and let his sister-in-law create a website for him using our templates, and he was so glad he did. His website hadn't been up for long when he contacted her to say he was getting enquiries through his website, and he was really chuffed about it. He could see then why his sister-in-law had been badgering him about it. The investment is worth it because work will come from a good website, and if you compare the cost of a website to how much each client is worth, especially for someone doing large projects like a builder, spending a bit of money on a decent website is a no brainer!

The Coach Who Had Tried to Do It All Herself

We work with a coach who works with women around confidence and anxiety, and she knew she should have a website because she kept hearing people say that, but she didn't really know how to use it.

She created her own website with information about what she did on there and tried to add in some courses and her book for people to buy, but it wasn't doing anything for her.

In this instance she didn't need a new website, the platform she was using was ok and easy to add new content to and the design wasn't too bad, it all just needed some serious tweaking. In short, she needed some professional guidance on the best tweaks to make.

We worked with her to make her page structure flow better, to make it clear to her website visitors what she did with an engaging statement at the top of her homepage. We also made sure she had clear call to action buttons so people could easily buy her book or get in touch to discuss working with her. We gave her all this advice, and best of all, she was a coach who was good at being coached. She listened, asked questions when she wasn't sure and then went away and made all the changes we suggested.

Once she'd made the changes she was really proud of her website, and she shared it on social media letting people know she had made some updates to her website and asked them what they thought. The next day she sold a copy of her book through her website and had an enquiry through her website that turned into a new client. The next day!!

When you have a website you are confident about and proud of, you're much more likely to share it with people. Having those clear call to action buttons on it allows you to ask for a sale without actually having to ask for it yourself. This is proof that you can create a decent website yourself, but not completely by yourself if that's not your area of expertise. Getting a professional involved to guide you or mentor you to make the most out of it is key to making it a good investment for your business.

The Stationery Business Who Needed Smartening Up

When you have a business where aesthetics and quality are important, this has to be reflected in your website. When the owner of a stationery company came to us saying she needed a new website, it was mainly because she felt her current one didn't reflect her brand.

In her business, she creates beautiful bespoke planners, diaries, and notebooks, as well as pretty gift boxes containing a range of stationery and complementary items. These are higher end products with a higher end price tag, so she wanted her website to reflect this.

Also, as an entrepreneur she wanted to be able to react to the needs of her clients and audience quickly and add new products to her website rapidly and easily when she saw an opportunity, and she wasn't finding this straightforward with her current website.

We thought it was great that she realised all of this needed to happen, what was even better is she knew that her time was better spent working on her business and her products than on her website, so she got us to create it for her. She understood and valued her time.

When her website went live, we emailed her to let her know, but she didn't see that email straight away. She realised her new website was live when she was alerted that she had made a sale through a notification on her phone. That was how quickly she made a sale, on the day her new website went live. While we'd been creating it we had taken her old website down, as we did with the construction company, because she was so unhappy with it and put up a holding page so people could contact her but couldn't buy through the website. Making a sale straight away made everything worthwhile for her and proved to her she'd taken the right step in improving her online space.

This could be you.

By the time you finish reading this book and using our tools we want you to have a story like theirs of first online enquiries, new leads, and easy sales. We know it's possible for all businesses, if they get their website right, if they invest in the right things!

WHAT A BUSINESS WEBSITE SHOULD DO

You can use the subtitles in this section almost as a checklist for when you've finished your website. But as time goes on, you can also use them to ensure your website is still doing what it should.

Establish You as An Expert

When someone is looking around your website it should be clear to them that you really are awesome at what you do. Sometimes people will hit your website cold, but most of the time they will have heard something about your business or seen you on social media and they're checking out your website to confirm that you're worth considering working with or buying from. This means your website has to prove that you are worth considering, demonstrating your expertise is one way of doing this.

Testimonials are a great way of proving that you really are good at what you do, because it's not just you saying it. Also, regular blog posts or articles about your area of business are a great way of showing your knowledge and providing something useful for your website visitor before they even become a client or customer.

Connect With Your Customer and Motivate Them to Work with You

To show someone that your business is the one they should be working with, you need to really connect with them. Your website copy needs to talk to them and show them that you understand their wants and needs and that you have a solution to the problem that led them to your website.

We always suggest that you have an engaging statement at the top of the homepage on your website which immediately shows your website visitor that they are in the right place. Some great examples of these are:

A stationery company who creates bespoke planners:

"Are you dreaming of finding the perfect planner that works for you?"

An author and film maker:

"My Life is Stories, Want to Hear More?"

A business coach in the fitness and wellness industry:

"Your GO TO place to grow your Fitness, Nutrition or Wellness business this year and beyond."

Straight away you know what these people do as soon as you see that statement on their website, you know you're in the right place and you do want to find out more.

Be Clear, Easy to Navigate and Easy to Read

Far too many websites have a really confusing layout, they look messy and cluttered and just create a terrible user experience. We recently heard one of our friends in the industry say that they were working with someone on their website and even they didn't know how to find something on there!

Websites like this often end up this way because they haven't been planned. As you are reading this book, you aren't going to have that problem! Also, we'll give you some great design tips later in the book to ensure it's easy for your website visitor to spot what they're looking for on each page and that they enjoy using the website.

Be Professional

It amazes us how often people who are really great at what they do, and want to be considered professionals in their field, have websites that are anything but professional. We've already talked about how a website is a reflection of you and your business, so it's key you make sure your reflection is looking good and performing well.

Work on Mobile Devices

This is hugely important. Over 50% of web browsing is done on a mobile phone, and Dave Chaffey[1] reported on Smart Insights in March 2021 that the Ericsson Mobility Report predicts a 25% increase in mobile traffic by 2025.

So, if your website doesn't work on a mobile device, you're missing out on reaching more than half of your potential future clients and customers.

Be an Extension of You and Your Brand

Every time somebody comes across you or your business it should be obvious to them that it's you. So if they see your branded vehicle or your social media presence and then visit your website, it should be clear that they're in the right place. Unfortunately this doesn't always happen because people forget about their website when they go through a rebrand, or they decide to create a really flashy, modern website and forget to create the same feel with their branding everywhere else. If your brand isn't consistent, you're giving your website visitor a jarring experience which will impact on how they feel when it comes to potentially buying from you.

Make It Easy to Build Your Email List

This is so important! Please do not rely on social media as a way of staying in touch with the people who are interested in what you do. You aren't in control of your social media. Not only is it oversaturated (so what you're saying doesn't stand out), but if you're unfortunate enough to have your account or page suspended or deleted, you really are a bit stuck. But if you have an email list, you are much more in control of how you communicate with and nurture your audience.

In their article, Email Marketing vs. Other Digital Marketing Channels[2], published in November 2018 and updated in July 2019, Campaign Monitor created a really interesting infographic comparing social media marketing with email marketing. The comparison which stood out the most to us was this:

> 30% of millennials engage with a brand on social media at least once a month (sourced from Social Sprout) vs. 73% of millennials identify email as their preferred means of business communication (sourced from WordStream).

A lot of people still want social media to be just that, social. We aren't saying not to use it, it's still a great tool to get in front of people, but to take the engagement to the next level, email is the way to go and using your website to build that email list is key.

Be Your Hub

Your website shouldn't just be about attracting your ideal client and generating leads and sales, although, that's a massive reason for having one. It should also make life easier for you. It should include all the answers to the questions that people ask you so you can send them to your website instead of answering the same question over and over. Your website should make taking payments easy. It should be a valuable business tool, your hub, and by it being your hub you will naturally drive traffic to it which is very important and something we'll talk more about later in the book.

CHAPTER 2
THE WEBSITE PLANNING PROCESS

THE IMPORTANCE OF PLANNING YOUR WEBSITE

A well-planned website will do so much more for your business than one that hasn't been well considered, hasn't been created with your specific business or client in mind and has basically just been thrown together. A well-planned website will create a lovely user experience for your website visitor. They'll know they've come to the right place as soon as they hit your website. Also, they'll be able to find everything they need easily and have all their questions answered without having to ask them.

Your website should be both the perfect first point of contact for your potential client and the sales convincer for people who already know a bit about you but wanted to do more research. If your website is already doing this, congratulations. If it's not, then here are the steps you should take to plan your website and create your website shopping list to help you choose the perfect option for creating your perfect website.

Below are the things you need to consider, in this order, when planning your website. This planning process will then inform your website shopping list, which will help you choose the right platform for your website. We've included our website planning worksheets in this section of the book, but if you'd rather not write in your book, you can download our Website Blueprint for free at this link so you can print it out: readysteadywebsites.com/handbook-resources/. If you are reading the print version of this book you may also like to get the download so you can see the images we use in colour.

YOUR IDEAL CLIENT

Firstly, you need to consider who your ideal client or customer is. This is important because you should have them in mind every step of the way when planning and creating your website. You should be thinking about the information they are going to want, the kinds of concerns or questions they might have, the kinds of images that will grab their attention, whether they have time to read long paragraphs of text or whether they're likely to appreciate to the point, snappy content. All of this will inform your website copy, the layout of your website, the images you choose and the next steps you put in front of visitors as calls to action.

Now it's time for your first task ...

Task: Identify Your Ideal Customer or Client

The first activity is to create your ideal customer or client avatar. You may already have done an activity similar to this before. If you have, great you have an advantage, but we recommend you revisit it and check that this is still how you view your ideal client.

Before you start your own customer avatar, check out our example which is coming up, to help you. Then use the worksheet on the page following the example to identify your own ideal client. Imagine your perfect customer and start writing – draw a little sketch too, even a stick person will help bring everything to life!

―――

TOP TIP for those just starting out ...

If you already have a very niche area that you work in and you're just starting your business, for example you are a nutritional therapist who works with people with autoimmune conditions, then you can make your customer avatar just that: someone with autoimmune problems. Then after you have been in business a while you might notice you are naturally attracting women with autoimmune conditions who are in their 30s and have children. At this point you should go through this customer avatar activity again, refine your customer avatar if needed and tweak your messaging.

―――

BRAND PERSONA & CUSTOMER AVATAR

EXAMPLE

FILL IN THE DETAILS, FILL THESE OUT WITH YOUR PERFECT CUSTOMER DETAILS NOT YOURS!

NAME: Jennifer
AGE: 39
CHILDREN? ☑ **HOW MANY?** 2 (5-11 yo)
MARRIED? ☑
JOB TITLE: Business Coach
LOCATION: UK

PERSONALITY TRAITS...
- Straight Talker
- Determined
- Focused
- Multi-tasker
- Ex corporate, used to high stress

GOALS & ASPIRATIONS...
- Wants freedom
- Life on my terms
- Money on my terms
- Passive income

CURRENT ISSUES...
- Not creative in business
- Too much working 1:1
- Always juggling: family, life, kids.
- "Tech" is a big blocker
- Makes £2k a month but needs to scale

SKETCH YOUR CUSTOMER

INTERESTS & HOBBIES...
- Running (loves it)
- Gym Classes

ANYTHING ELSE?...
- Has a VA
- Works from home
- Not sure if her brand + website truly resonates with customers
- Hates Brexit
- Disillusioned with politics

😞 PROBLEMS, CHALLENGES & PAIN POINTS

- Hates tech, doesn't have a clue how to make it all work together
- Got 'screwed' over in the past with her website
- Desperately wants to leverage tech & websites to automate her workflow
- Wants to create something truly scaleable
- Wants some future proof built in

😊 POSITIVES, WHAT IS WORKING RIGHT NOW

- Knows that if she finds the right person that the tech will all come together
- Has a great record in her 1:1 work
- Her customers love her & rave about her!
- She has freedom already (but would like more)
- She feels like she is achieving for herself rather than a faceless company now

… 19

BRAND PERSONA & CUSTOMER AVATAR

FILL IN THE DETAILS, FILL THESE OUT WITH YOUR PERFECT CUSTOMER DETAILS NOT YOURS!

NAME: _____
AGE: ____
CHILDREN? ☐ HOW MANY? _____
MARRIED? ☐
JOB TITLE: _____
LOCATION: _____

PERSONALITY TRAITS…

GOALS & ASPIRATIONS…

INTERESTS & HOBBIES…

ANYTHING ELSE?…

CURRENT ISSUES…

SKETCH YOUR CUSTOMER

☹ PROBLEMS, CHALLENGES & PAIN POINTS   ☺ POSITIVES, WHAT IS WORKING RIGHT NOW

Talking to your customer's pain points

Now that you have a clear picture of your customer, it's time to start talking to those pain points. Not in a scary fear-mongering kind of way, but so that you are able to empathise with the pain points and offer a direct solution for each. This will help you with creating your content when we get to that.

Pain Point	Your Solution
Example.. *PAIN POINT #1* *Hates tech, doesn't have a clue how to make it all work together.*	*We make tech easy with our simple tutorials and easy to use Page Builder.*
Example.. *PAIN POINT #1* *Hates tech, doesn't have a clue how to make it all work together.*	

THE PURPOSE OF YOUR WEBSITE

Now that you know who your ideal client is, you know who you are creating your website for. Next, you need to think about your website's purpose. By purpose we mean what you want your website visitor to do while they are there. Do you want to make direct sales through your website? Get people to join your membership? Or do you like to have a chat with your potential client first to see if they are the right fit for your service? If so, the purpose would be to get them to get in touch via a contact form or to book in for a call through a calendar link. Whatever the purpose is, you need to keep it in mind when you're writing your content and planning the structure of your website so that you lead that website visitor to taking the desired action.

Donald Miller writes brilliantly about this side of planning your website in his book *Building a Story Brand*[1]. He says you should have both a primary purpose and secondary purpose for your website. The primary purpose is what we've just mentioned. The secondary purpose is a backup so that you can still get a lead from your website, even if they aren't ready to commit to buying from you yet. This is when it's great to have an option for your website visitor to join your email list, subscribe to your blog or join a community you have on social media. This way you have brought them into your world, they can get to know you better, and down the line, when they are ready to commit to spending the money, you are the person they will do it with.

Here's another task for you...

Task: The Purpose of Your Website

Now have a think about what it is you want your website to achieve. As an example, the primary purpose of our website is to get people to join Ready Steady Websites® – to actually hit the join now button and spend money through the site. The secondary purpose is to encourage people to make contact with us in some way, whether that's chatting to us through the chat function, signing up for a call or joining our email list by downloading one of our free resources. It's a step to us building a relationship so hopefully down the line they will hit the join now button – back to the primary function.

Use the following space to identify the purpose of your website and your thought process behind it as we have done in our example above. Knowing what you want your website to achieve will help you plan and create the content to achieve this purpose.

Primary purpose of my website:

Secondary purpose of my website:

How this secondary purpose will support the primary purpose:

DOING YOUR RESEARCH

It's a really good idea to do some research into other websites. This will give you a good sense of some of the design elements you'd like on your website, the functionality you'll need and the type of language that is used on other websites in your area of industry. You'll see the benefit of this when it comes to creating your website shopping list, which is the document you will use to inform your choice of website platform – you really want to get that right first time!

Obviously, you need to take action to do research, so we have another task for you!

Task: Doing Your Research

Use these pages to help you get a good idea of what you want your ideal website to look like.

Do a bit of research by looking at websites of companies that you use regularly and think about what it is about their website that makes you their visitor or customer. Try to look at three different examples.

Then, visit the websites of your competitors. What is it that you think works on their websites? What doesn't work?

Are there any other websites that inspire you?

Are there any websites that you have visited before that you really didn't like, or you thought just didn't work? Go back and have another look at them and work out why that is.

Note down the findings of your research on the next pages.

Your Research Notes

The Websites You Use Regularly

Website name:

Your thoughts from your research:

Website name:

Your thoughts from your research:

Website name:

Your thoughts from your research:

Your Competitors

Website name:

Your thoughts from your research:

Website name:

Your thoughts from your research:

Website name:

Your thoughts from your research:

Other Websites That Inspire You

Website name:

Your thoughts from your research:

Website name:

Your thoughts from your research:

Website name:

Your thoughts from your research:

Websites You Really Don't Like

Website name:

Your thoughts from your research:

Website name:

Your thoughts from your research:

Website name:

Your thoughts from your research:

What's next?

Looking back through your notes, try to see if there are any recurring themes across the websites you have visited. Using these common themes, identify the following.

Three things you think work well on a website and would attract customers, e.g. well laid out.

1. _____
2. _____
3. _____

Three things you would definitely avoid using on your website.

1. _____
2. _____
3. _____

Note down any design styles / trends / layouts you would consider using on your website.

1. _____
2. _____
3. _____

CREATING YOUR WEBSITE SITEMAP

It's important at the early stage of your website planning to think about your sitemap, which includes the pages you'll have on your website and how they link together. By doing this, you'll create a strong journey that flows through your website. It will also help you write your content in a methodical way by approaching it one page at a time.

We have some top tips to follow when creating your sitemap, but here are two key rules to follow:

1. Ideally, you should have no more than eight menu items in your main menu (or navigation as it's also referred to).

2. The main purpose of your website should be achieved in no more than three clicks from the homepage.

You should keep to eight menu items or fewer because giving your website visitor too much choice about which pages to look at can overwhelm them. As a result, they might not click on anything, or they might take a long time to find the right page. Also, it looks very cluttered if you have a lot of menu items along the top of the homepage or in a drop-down menu on mobile. Clutter causes confusion and indecision.

Keep your main-purpose action within three clicks of the home page and by this we mean actually clicking the buy button on a product or booking a call as the third click. The more pages and clicks you add in, the more likely it is that your potential customer will give up. You want them to take quick decisive action.

So, let's get to planning your website layout with the next task …

Task: Creating Your Sitemap

To create your sitemap you'll need some sticky notes and a pen, or perhaps a few pens in different colours. Use the guide, which is coming up, to get started on the three parts of this task.

This activity is really useful whether you have a website already or not. If you do already have a website, try to put your current sitemap out of your head. Instead, imagine you are starting from scratch and really think about your website visitor's journey. It will be interesting to see how much difference there is between what you come up with today and what you already have.

What A Sitemap Looks Like

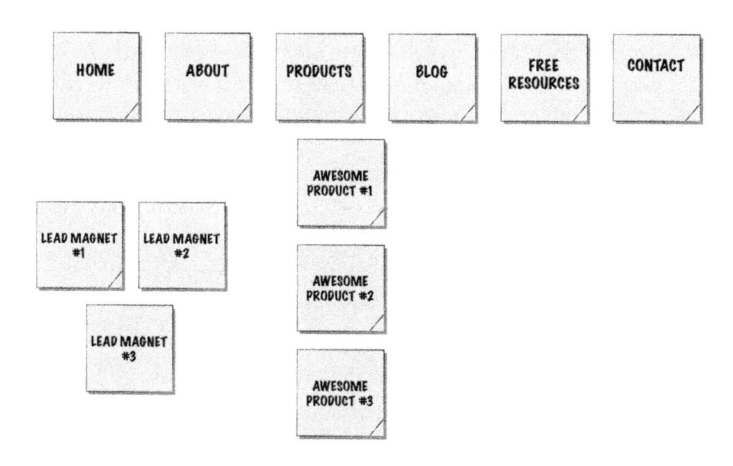

This is a very basic example of a sitemap. The sticky notes across the top are the pages that would appear in the top navigation or menu of the website. The products numbered 1-3 would be on the product page or could be in a drop-down menu from the products menu item in the main navigation as they look in the photo.

The three lead magnets off to the side would be stand-alone pages (lead magnets are free downloads or offers you create and provide in exchange for an email address). In this example, they would be there on the website, but they would only be accessed via a direct link such as a link from a Facebook post. They wouldn't appear in the navigation at all. On your website you may want to have your lead magnets in the navigation, on a free resources page or dotted around your content, that's also fine.

So, let's put this into practice.

What pages do you need?

Think about the pages you need on your website. Perhaps think about the websites you researched to help you do this. Write a post it note for each page you want on your website.

Get sticking

Stick your sticky notes on the wall in the way you think you would like the pages laid out on your website. Before you do this, consider the two top tips we mentioned, which we have highlighted below again. Also, remember to consider what you thought about the websites you looked at in your research.

TOP TIP #1

You shouldn't have more than eight menu items in your top navigation or main menu. Eight is the absolute maximum. We would recommend trying to stick to six or fewer. Too many options make your menu will look cluttered, and it will be difficult for your website visitor to see what they're looking for.

TOP TIP #2

Everything on your website should be no more than three clicks away for your website visitor. Using the sitemap in the photo, if they arrive on the homepage, their first click is on the products menu item, their second click is on product they like, their third click is to buy it. That's nice and easy for them. They're still interested when they see the buy button. Any more than that and they might give up.

Does it flow?

Once you've completed your sitemap, take a step back and have a look at it. Does it flow nicely for the website visitor? Is everything within three clicks?

Additional Essential Pages

There are some other pages that you must have on your website to cover you legally. The laws that you are governed by will vary depending on where you're based, so you need to do your own research to find out what you must legally have on your website.

In the UK, these are the three documents you must have on your website:

1. a website terms of use,
2. a privacy policy and
3. a cookie policy.

You should also have a way for visitors to opt into your cookies – yes this means one of those cookie pop ups, sorry!

Usually, people create a simple web page for each of these and link to them from a menu in the footer of their website. If you're selling goods or services through your website, you'll also need specific terms and conditions related to those products or services.

If at any point your website visitor is giving you personal information or making a payment, they need to tick a box to say they agree to your terms and have read your policies. If they are joining your email list, they have to tick to show they are actively opting into the list, You cannot have the box pre-ticked.

We are not legal experts. We strongly recommend you get legal advice on what you need on your own website to ensure you comply with any legal requirements for your industry and location. We aren't saying this to scare you; it is very simple, and many experts have templates you can use to create these documents to make it nice and easy.

WRITING YOUR CONTENT

Once you've decided on the pages you're going to have on your website, you need to plan what you're going to have on them. We advise that you lead with writing your content. Content is key when it comes to your website. Your content delivers the message that you want to convey to your ideal client. This is so important. You should create your content in a way that gets your message across and then choose a template design or have a website designed based on the content you have.

Here's a task to help you get started …

Task: Writing Your Content

Use this section to help you write the copy for your website. The following exercise outlines the things you need to consider when creating your website copy, and there is a worksheet to help you structure it.

Your Content

All of your content should be written with your customer in mind. What do they want? How do you want them to feel? What information do you need to convey to entice, excite and get them to click that call to action?

Even if you don't feel confident writing and think it might

be better to get someone else to write your website copy for you, you are the one who truly knows your business, so you should take the first stab at what content should go on each page.

Tone of Voice & Language

It is really important that your content speaks to your target audience (or customer avatar). Make sure you don't use any technical jargon, unless appropriate, and ensure you use content that resonates with your audience.

At all points, the audience should feel like they are having a conversation with you and getting to know you better. You should be building their trust and confidence at every touch point with your brand.

The easiest way to do this is to not overthink it. Be you, be authentic and remain consistent with the way you write blog posts, Facebook posts and website copy.

Also, focus on the primary objective for each webpage. A homepage will likely have a summary theme of what you can help your ideal client with, explanation of who you are and something to entice people to click through and dig deeper. An about page will be more in depth, building trust and connection. A sales page will be more persuasive and more focused on the person taking action, getting them all excited to take the next step.

Calls to Action

Getting your calls to action right are key in making your website successful at generating leads and sales. They link into the purpose of your website and will normally be buttons that you want your website visitor to click on the get them to "Sign Up", "Join Now", or "Buy Now".

Your calls to action need to actually say what they are going to do. If your button is going to send your website visitor off to book a call, have the words "Book a Call" on the button. Don't have the words "Get in Touch" or "Contact Us" on the button. Those words imply that they are going to be taken to a contact page with a choice of contact methods or perhaps a contact form. It's a jarring experience for someone to expect that but then to be faced with booking a call. It feels a bit underhanded and pressurised, and people will be put off by that.

The whole website experience needs to flow nicely with no unexpected outcomes. When it does, your website visitor is much more likely to take a positive action.

Let's map it out

Use the upcoming worksheet as a content template for each page of your website.

Before you begin ...

- Check out the following example for how to map your content.
- Check out the visual example after that for how that content can transfer into a designed web page.
- Start to think about images you want to use for each section of content (we'll cover image selection and usage in more detail later on).

and ...

- You don't have to write ALL of your content into the worksheet, you can use the worksheet as a bullet point list, so you know what you want to

cover in each section and write that up in more detail in a separate Word document. You may already have a vision of how you want each webpage to look, so you may need more sections or fewer depending on what content you want to write on each page. That's all completely cool, this is your website.
- Make sure you don't overcomplicate things. Keep it succinct and "on point" – directed at your ideal customer avatar.

38 THE WEBSITE HANDBOOK

EXAMPLE

Page Name: *Homepage*

Goal for page: *Contact me*
e.g. Sign up to My Club, Contact me, Get free download

PRIMARY SECTION HEADING *Amanda Smith – Life Coach*

PRIMARY SECTION CONTENT:

I'm good at what I do, I've helped hundreds of people get their life in order personally and professionally. If you're a female entrepreneur who wants to take their life to the next level then we should have a chat... like now!

RELEVANT IMAGERY? ☑   CALL TO ACTION NEEDED? ☑   WILL THIS MAKE SENSE TO MY AUDIENCE? ☑

SECONDARY SECTION HEADING *Live your best life*

SECONDARY SECTION CONTENT:

My brand new programme is designed to take you from overwhelmed & confused to having a clear direction and goals that you are achieving to get there. Programme launches in 60 days. Sign up here!

☑   ☑   ☑

CONTENT FOR OTHER ELEMENTS OF THE PAGE
e.g. On a home page you may have a services panel and want to showcase 3 services or a free download panel

Clarity Call	Amanda Action Time	Amanda A-Team
Free, no commitment chat with me.	Book in for a £99 action plan with me.	VIP membership for £299 a month
☐ ☑ ☑	☐ ☑ ☑	☐ ☑ ☑

THE WEBSITE PLANNING PROCESS 39

Here is an example of how the worksheet can help you visualise your final webpage layout. You don't always need every single element, and you can add more elements or mix and match elements too.

Primary Section Heading
Primary Section Content
Primary Call to Action Button
Secondary Call to Action Button

Content for other elements

Secondary Section Heading
Secondary Section Content

Secondary / Alternate Section Call to Action

40 THE WEBSITE HANDBOOK

Use the following content planning sheet for each page on your website. As we mentioned you can download our Website Blueprint (readysteadywebsites.com/handbook-resources/), so you can print this page out as many times as you need for all the pages on your website.

Page Name: _____ **Goal for page:** _____
e.g. Sign up to My Club, Contact me, Get free download

PRIMARY SECTION HEADING _____

PRIMARY SECTION CONTENT:

RELEVANT IMAGERY? ☐   CALL TO ACTION NEEDED? ☐   WILL THIS MAKE SENSE TO MY AUDIENCE? ☐

SECONDARY SECTION HEADING _____

SECONDARY SECTION CONTENT:

☐   ☐   ☐

CONTENT FOR OTHER ELEMENTS OF THE PAGE
e.g. On a home page you may have a services panel and want to showcase 3 services or a free download panel

☐ ☐ ☐   ☐ ☐ ☐   ☐ ☐ ☐

CREATING WIREFRAMES (PAGE LAYOUT)

Another thing you might find useful is to sketch a "wireframe" of how you would like each page of your website to look to help you plan out the copy you would like on each page.

Wireframing is a way of sketching and planning out your website pages. This is a great way to get all the page layouts and text, as well as video and image placement mapped out without getting bogged down with the pretty design aspects. It will also help you shape the functionality you want your website to have. For example: Do you need a search box? Do you want a map? Do you want a video? etc.

THE WEBSITE HANDBOOK

This is an example of a wireframe:

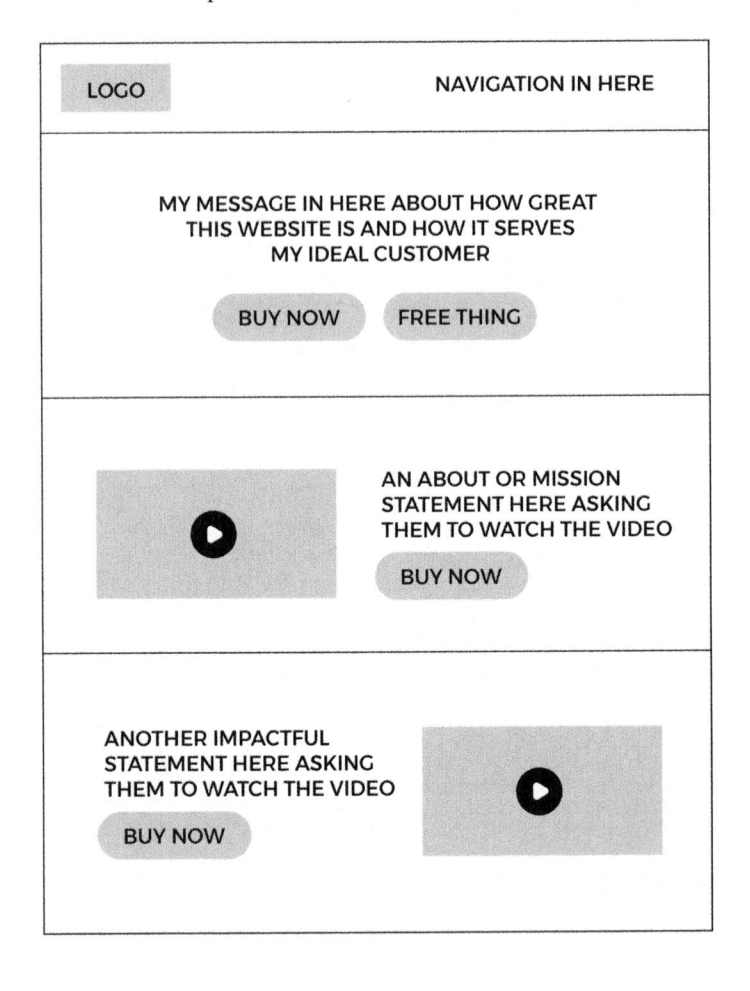

PLANNING AND SOURCING YOUR IMAGES

Images make or break a website. You can have the most perfectly planned website, with a fantastic layout, beautifully written copy that speaks directly to the website visitor and calls to action that stand out and reflect the purpose of your website, but if your website visitor is faced with dull, unprofessional, uninspiring images, they probably won't even stick around to find out how awesome everything else on your website is.

We cannot stress this enough – if you have the budget, invest in professional photography. Have a personal brand shoot or product shoot and discuss with your photographer all the images you'll need for your website so they properly fit in with your content and your layout to create a cohesive experience.

If your budget doesn't stretch to a professional shoot, then invest in a course to teach you how to take amazing product photography and how to set up your phone or camera to take great heads shots. It is amazing how good the photos can be that you take yourself with the right guidance.

After that, stock photography is an OK option, but you need to make sure you choose well, check the licensing on the images that you want to use, and if possible use stock photography sites where you can choose images from the same shoot or the same photographer so that you get a really consistent feel across your website – just as you would with photos from your own shoot.

Task: Planning and Sourcing Your Images

An awesome image is eye catching and inspiring, and it draws your website visitor in. A terrible image can make them take one look and leave the website.

The Professional route

If you think some professional photos are the way to go, we suggest you research some photographers. It's always best to get recommendations from other business friends but do contact a few and have a chat with them. Why? Because you want to get on with them and have a good feeling about them so you'll feel at ease when having your photo taken. If you don't, it will show in the photos. Even if it's a product shoot, it can take a while. Also, you want to be on the same wavelength so that your products are showcased in a way that you are happy with.

You'll need to have an idea of the images that you want when you meet with your photographer for the first time. Have a look at your wireframes or the page templates that you identified. Use these to help you create a list of the photos that you need taken.

Also consider whether you need any photos that will have text over the top of them so that space can be left in the photos for this. Now, using the following table, write a list of the photos you need and the page you'll put them on.

Website Page	Photos Needed

Free stock photography route

If you're on a tight budget, you can go with stock photos. Just be really picky about which ones you choose and make sure they convey your message. Ensure they support a natural progression from you, your brand and the tone of voice you have instilled into your content. Wherever possible, try to pick ones you think don't look like a stock photo.

Using your wireframes, choose the images you need for

each page from these stock photography sites and save them into a folder on your computer ready to use on your website.

Check out the list below!

Copyright and Creative Commons

Before we get started, here is a quick disclaimer. Most of these image websites provide completely free to use images. However, some of them come with restrictions under Creative Commons licences. There are different types of Creative Commons licences, some give you 100% rights over the image, some require attribution for use, and some completely prohibit commercial use, so please be diligent and double-check with the website author or image copyright holder to make sure.

1. **Unsplash (unsplash.com)** This is our favourite free stock photo website. It is quite "hipster" but also has some great generic, abstract and mouth-wateringly good food images. The only drawback of this website is that it is very popular, so if you're looking for originality you may want to continue down this list.
2. **FoodiesFeed (foodiesfeed.com)** If you're a foodie, you need to check it out.
3. **Picjumbo (picjumbo.com)** We're getting a little bit more "stock like" now, but there are some great finds in picjumbo if you are willing to browse through their catalogue.
4. **StockSnap (stocksnap.io)** has a real jumble of great quality images and poor quality ones, but it's always worth a flick through as there they have some lovely photos.
5. **Gratis Photography (gratisography.com)** There are some truly bizarre photos on Gratis

Photography, but it's a great place to go if you're looking for a specific or niche image.
6. **Free Range Stock (freerangestock.com)** This really is a free version of popular "stock photo" websites. Free Range has some awesomely cheesy photos, but there are a few gems to be uncovered too.
7. **Pexels (pexels.com)** This one has a complete mix-up of those cheesy stock photos and high quality shots, worth a browse for sure.
8. **New Old Stock (nos.twnsnd.co)** Much like old written publications and books, old photos are sometimes also free from copyright. New Old Stock holds a small archive of these. It's a bit niche, but there are a few lovely original shots in there that could provide the originality your quality blog post is asking for.
9. **Pixabay (pixabay.com)** There are some great natural, nature based and wildlife images on pixabay. It is a great place to go if you're looking for some scenery shots, landscape photos or the obligatory cute kitten!

THE IMPORTANCE OF BRAND CONSISTENCY

We've mentioned brand a couple of times in this section of the book, and it's important enough to explain in more detail here. Why? Because it's vital to all areas of your business, including and especially on your website.

You need a good, professional brand that truly reflects you or your business but that will also appeal to your ideal customer or client. Your brand includes your logo, your colours, your fonts but also your tone of voice, the message you put out there about what you do, and the way you present yourself and your services or products. These are all part of your brand and it's important that all of these things are consistent at every touch point someone has with you or your business.

This level of consistency is important because a lack of consistency can create a jarring experience for a potential customer or client, and then they are less likely to feel confident buying from you. Imagine you are doing really well on social media: you've got up to date photos on there, your branding looks great, and you're talking the talk really well, so someone decides to head on over to your website. They see a picture of someone they don't recognise from your socials because it's a 20-year-old photo. You don't have any evidence of current work on there. Your site is still using your old logo, and it basically looks like you have forgotten about your business. That person is going to wonder whether what you are putting on social media is really happening and whether you can really walk the walk.

As we said at the start of the book, many people tell us that they don't even consider buying from a business until they have checked out their website, so you really need it to be delivering the same brand experience as everything else you are doing in your business.

CREATING YOUR WEBSITE SHOPPING LIST

Now it's time to create your shopping list! Use the guidance below and the next task to help you.

Functionality

It's really important to be clear on the functionality that you need for your website because this is one of the areas that is going to be the most influential in deciding on the platform that you will use for creating it. You should take some time to consider the purpose of your website and then think about what you need your website to do to achieve that purpose. These are some things to think about:

- If you want to sell products, then you need an online shop or ecommerce website.
- If you want people to pay for your services, you need to be able to take payments.
- If you'd like people to book a call, you need to be able to link to a calendar booking system.
- If you're going to build an email list and have an email system that you'd like to use, then the platform you choose needs to be compatible with this.

The list could go on and on. Make sure you take a lot of time to think about it, otherwise you'll be frustrated if you're halfway through creating your website and then realise you can't do something.

Also, if you have an idea but haven't seen a platform that does it, still write it down. It possibly has been done before, but if not, someone can probably create it for you.

Plan for Now and the Future

When you're considering everything that you need on your website, think about your functionality requirements and even design elements that you like now and also what you might need in the future. For example, at the moment you may have a service based business, but you are interested in launching a product range that supports your service in the next couple of years. At that point, you'll need an online shop. Make sure you write "online shop" down on your list.

The reason we encourage you to plan for the future is that creating a website takes time, effort, and money, so you really only want to do it once. Investing in a website on a platform that you won't grow out of is a really good idea. Doing so will allow your website to grow with your business without having to start from scratch a few years down the line.

This is where getting into an investing mindset really is key. If you are new to business, it's very easy to think that as your business is new, you don't want to pay too much money for a website; something cheaper is fine for now. But, if you go cheap and take an "it'll do approach" now, then we almost guarantee you'll end up spending more money in the long run. Also, as we've said before, you'll get far more work from a really good website and then the investment will pay off.

Task: Website Shopping List

This is where you pull everything together that we've considered so far in order to create a shopping list of all the design elements and functionality that you need or want on your website. Take a look at the research you did, your sitemap, and your wireframes and use all of that to create your list.

We've provided worksheets for you to use to create your list and also provided two example lists to help you.

EXAMPLE

Immediate requirements

1. Large hero image area at the top of each page
2. Sign up box in footer
3. Landing pages for lead magnets
4. Map on contact us/find us page
5. Videos in blog
6. Link to Calendly to book client meetings
7.
8.
9.
10.

Future requirements

1. Sales pages for retreats
2. Sales page for membership
3. Private membership site or area
4. Connect to Stripe to take payments
5. Somewhere to put free webinars
6. A team page
7.
8.
9.
10.

Immediate requirements

1. _____
2. _____
3. _____
4. _____
5. _____
6. _____
7. _____
8. _____
9. _____
10. _____

Future requirements

1. _____
2. _____
3. _____
4. _____
5. _____
6. _____
7. _____
8. _____
9. _____
10. _____

CHAPTER 3
CHOOSING YOUR PLATFORM AND SUPPORTING TECH

When it comes to choosing the platform to create your website on or the method for creating it, most people tend to take completely the wrong approach. They don't do any of the planning that we've been through; they don't make a list of functionality or design features that they need or would like. The first thing they do is go on to social media and type, "I need a website, what did you use to make yours?"

This is probably one of the least useful things you can do because the responses you are going to get will look something like this:

- I used Wix but wouldn't recommend it.
- I used Squarespace, really easy to use.
- I used Wix and really like it.
- I use Kajabi.
- I use Squarespace, but I'm thinking of moving.
- WordPress and Divi, love it.
- I think Elementor's better than Divi.
- Talk to Jude at Ready Steady Websites®; they're great.

- My brother in law did mine. Let me know if you want his details.
- I do websites; I'll DM you.

Now, that really isn't helpful. All you've found out from that is that everyone has a different experience and opinion. Also, following such a post, you'll probably get bombarded with unsolicited messages from web designers with no social media etiquette. Obviously not from Jude at Ready Steady Websites®!

But you aren't going to panic and ask silly questions on social media because you've gone through the planning process: you have your website shopping list at the ready, and you can use that to help you pick the right platform.

In the following task, we highlight the types of website platforms that are out there, and we name some of the bigger players of each of the types. We highlight some of the pros and cons of each platform type and also do a price comparison, because price is a factor when choosing your platform, especially as for some of them you'll be tied in financially for the life of your website.

So, let's take a closer look at the platforms.

WEBSITE PLATFORM OPTION COMPARISONS

Task: Choosing Website Platform Options

There are more website, membership site, landing page and learning management systems than you can shake a stick at – not that you'd want to shake a stick at them, because that would be well ... a bit pointless!

This is an overview of the different types of options out there. We don't exhaustively list every single system out there, but we give a brief overview of what to expect from each "type" of platform.

TOP TIP Don't jump ahead!...

Before we look at the options, make sure you haven't jumped ahead – have you actually done the following?

Planned your website

In planning your site, you'll identify everything you need and want from your website. This helps you create your "website shopping list". You know this because you've read the book so far!

Created your website shopping list for now and the future

This depends on what your business plans are and where you're planning to take your business. If you don't do this, you may regret it down the line when you're having to invest more time and money, starting from scratch on a different system or platform.

The information on the next page will be most useful if you consider it alongside your website shopping list.

The Platforms

There are so many website platforms out there and they vary in what they provide, so let's break it down into platform "type" first.

Website & Ecommerce Services
Prices range from £0 TO £300 PM (per month)

Squarespace, Wix, Weebly, and WordPress.com are all

popular website services, and they also do ecommerce (online shops). Shopify is specifically for ecommerce but does some of the standard "website" things too.

These kinds of systems are often referred to as SaaS – Software as a Service. This means they manage everything – web hosting, uptime, site speed, support, and sometimes even your domain name. This makes things easy to get started, but it does leave a lot of the power and ownership with the platform provider.

For example, all of your content is on their servers – if you fail to pay or close your account, you'll lose that content. They don't have offsite backups that you have access to, meaning should something go wrong down the line, you will not have a backup of your site anywhere other than on their servers. They are also in control of your website speed – as everything is on their servers, there are some elements from a server perspective you will just not be able to speed up.

On all of the above services, you sign up and pay them a monthly or annual fee, you use their services on their web hosting and servers to create your website. The more functionality you want, the more expensive it tends to get.

Pros	Cons
· Easy to get going · Don't have to worry about hosting · Good support from some, although it can be hit and miss · Good website uptime	· Limited functionality · Difficult to create something unique · Most people outgrow them within 18 months · All your content is on their servers · No automated way of externally backing up your data/site · No way of optimising performance · You will be paying for the entire duration of having your website, the monthly or yearly cost never goes down.

Landing Pages & Funnels
Prices range from £80 TO £250 PM

LeadPages and Clickfunnels make it quick and easy to create simple landing pages where people can opt in to receive your freebie, and they connect to your email system (like Mailchimp, Active Campaign etc.). Clickfunnels goes a few steps further and allows you to create multi-page website "funnels" where people can opt in to your freebie or buy a product. Much like the website services, you sign up and pay them a monthly or annual fee; you use their services on their web hosting and servers to create your content.

Again, these are SaaS platforms, as we talked about in the previous section.

At the time of writing, Clickfunnels looks set to also become an all-in-one platform (which we'll talk about soon) during 2022, so look out for that!

Pros	Cons
· Don't have to worry about hosting · Great for ad campaigns · Good support · Good uptime	· There is a learning curve to understanding the system · Very much designed for opt in pages and campaigns · Cannot create a fully functioning website · US centric – if using payment systems, there are no built-in tax options · Severely limited page builder · No way of optimising performance · All your content is on their servers · No automated way of externally backing up your data/site · You will be paying for the entire duration of having your website; the monthly or yearly cost never goes down.

Learning Management & Membership Systems
Prices range from £0 TO £350 PM

Teachable & Thinkific are learning management systems and more recently membership systems. There are new learning management platforms coming out on almost a daily basis, including but not limited to New Zenler, Podia and MemberVault.

These types of platforms are only going to be useful to you if you're selling a membership or courses, but as you might have identified that functionality on your shopping list, we wanted to mention them.

Again, these are SaaS platforms, and everything sits on their hosting and services; you pay a monthly or annual fee to host your courses and/or membership on their platform.

Pros	Cons
· Easy to get going · Designed for courses predominantly and can also run memberships · Don't have to worry about hosting · Good support · Good uptime	· Difficult to create full websites on them · US centric – if using payment systems there are no built-in tax options · No way of optimising performance · All your content is on their servers · No automated way of externally backing up your data/site · You will be paying for the entire duration of having your website; the monthly or yearly cost never goes down.

All-in-one Services
Prices Range from £80 TO £450 PM

Kajabi and Kartra (and most probably Clickfunnels will join this list later in 2022) boast a powerful feature set. With these systems you don't need anything else. Your email system is with them, as well as your website, your membership site, and your courses.

The idea is that they are "all-in-one". Which means they are designed to take away the need for other platforms: websites, funnels, email marketing, membership, learning management, ecommerce. Everything goes through them, which as we're sure you can imagine is both amazing and not so amazing at the same time.

It's amazing because everything in one place, but it's not so amazing as it comes with a price tag. Also, if your access goes wrong, you miss a payment or the service goes down, you'll lose access to everything while you resolve it. No website will have perfect up time, but usually when it's down you can send out an email apologising; this doesn't work if your emails are down at the same time.

Pros	Cons
· Designed to work as a fully integrated system · Don't have to worry about hosting · Good support · Good uptime	· Expensive · All your "eggs" are in their "basket" – for example if the whole system goes down you can't email people · No way of optimising performance · All your content is on their servers · No automated way of externally backing up your data/site · Limited functionality · Steep learning curve · You will be paying for the entire duration of having your website; the monthly or yearly cost never goes down.

WordPress (self-hosted)
Prices range from £10PM TO ENTIRELY CUSTOM

WordPress has a self-hosted version where the platform can be installed on a web server. For WordPress (self-hosted) to work, you need a domain name and web hosting.

What is a domain name?
A domain name is your web address, like readysteadywebsites.com – this is what people type in or click on to visit your website. You'll need a domain name for all of the platforms.

What is web hosting?
Your web hosting is where your website lives. Your website is essentially a number of files and a database on a computer called a server. That server is where your website is hosted, and it sits in a network of lots of other servers. Then when someone types your website address or domain name into a web browser or clicks on a link, they are sent to those files and database on the server and your website shows. Web hosting isn't a requirement on the SaaS platforms.

WordPress is the most popular content management system in the world. It powers over 43% of the internet. According to Kinsta.com[1] in 2020, 500+ sites are built each day using WordPress while only 60–80 per day are built on platforms like Shopify and Squarespace.

WordPress's plugin ecosystem makes it a very extendable platform. Want a shop? Install WooCommerce. Want a membership site? Install MemberPress. The list goes on with 55,000+ plugins available for WordPress.

You can create anything you could possibly imagine through WordPress. You can start off on a really low budget and easily "plug in" extra functionality as you grow.

Pros	Cons
· You have complete control · Can be done on a really tight budget · Can easily be extended · You can create whatever you want with WordPress · Powers over 40% of the web · Easy to use · Developers love it so you'll always be able to find support if needed	· No support in its own right (but there are many services that will support you with WordPress)
	Past Cons
	· Bad reputation of being hard to use (which isn't the case anymore) · Bad reputation for security (WordPress is the most highly tested platform out there and is actually very secure)

WordPress self-hosted is our personal preference, and that is what we create all of our websites with. If you are going to use it, we recommend you use a service that creates a website on WordPress that also offers guidance and support. You can find lots of WordPress training materials out there for free but having someone to go to when you need to ask questions is so valuable, especially if creating a website is new to you.

However, as great as we think WordPress is, it needs to be a good fit for you. Which is why we give you the tools to do your own research and build your own shopping list of requirements. Ultimately, the choice is down to you and should be dictated by what you know you need right now and what you plan to add to your website in the future.

WEBSITE PLATFORM PRICES

We have given you a guide on price range for each of the platform types. The prices for each method of creating a website vary massively depending on the package you go for. For a business website, we wouldn't recommend you even consider the totally free options because they don't include some things, such as analytics, which are important when you're trying to ensure your website is attracting the right people and motivating them to click through to the pages you want them to be looking at. The free versions also tend to be heavily and obviously branded with the platform logo and name … not a great look for a professional business.

You also need to take into consideration hidden costs such as additional transaction fees. Stripe or PayPal already take a transaction fee, so you don't really want to choose a website platform that adds another one on top of that. Squarespace adds in transaction fees on some of its cheaper plans and so does Shopify.

The lower end cost for WordPress (self-hosted) that we have given is purely based on web hosting. WordPress itself is free but you will have to host it and pay for a domain name.

THE OPTION OF GETTING IT DONE FOR YOU

It may well be that you have a completely custom idea or part of your idea is completely custom, and you'll need to get someone to either design or build your website for you. You need to make sure you choose a genuine designer or developer to do this. Unfortunately there are people out there who claim to be web developers, but actually they are just quite good at using a platform and don't really have any development knowledge or experience. We have put this list together to make sure you don't get caught out.

Here are some red flags to look out for ...

- **They don't have a portfolio:** They should have a website showcasing their work.
- **They have no testimonials, reviews, or past clients that you're able to talk to:** They should have testimonials on their website or past clients you are able to contact.
- **All of their past projects look the same:** They may

be using a $50 theme and making some minor modifications but charging thousands – which is not cool.
- **When you ask questions, their answers are vague:** Any web designer or developer who knows their craft will be passionate about their work and able to explain in detail.
- **They don't have a clear process:** They should be able to explain what happens when you work with them, typical timeframes, and an idea of when a project would start with them.
- **They are charging you 100% upfront:** If we had a £1 for every time someone came to us who had paid 100% upfront for their website and then the web designer/developer has not delivered, we'd be rich by now. It happens all the time – DO NOT pay 100% upfront.
- **They have no actual web development experience:** This happens all the time too, you hire a web designer, but they can't develop. They are limited by the theme or plugins they use. If you're going custom, they should have web development and coding experience. So ask them about the code they know.
- **They have no contract you can sign:** They should give you a simple professional contract, an outline of the project and costs that you both sign.
- **They offer to buy your domain name:** You should own your domain name; it is your IP and no one else should have control over it. Your web designer should want you to own it too. You need to be in control of that.

OTHER TECH TO CONSIDER

Email Marketing System

Unless you decide to go all in with one of the all-in-one systems, you will need an email marketing system so you can build your email list and send out automated and scheduled emails. There are lots out there, but if you're just getting started, we recommend you take a look at Mailerlite, Convertkit, Campaign Monitor or Active Campaign.

At the time of writing, you can get started for free on Mailerlite with up to 1000 subscribers and on Convertkit with up to 300 subscribers. Then after that all of their basic plans come in around the $10 mark. Prices will then increase depending on the size of your email list and the number of emails you're sending out.

To decide which one is right for you, have a look at the functionality they each offer and the support they provide. Crucially, make sure they're compatible with the website platform you have chosen to use.

Calendar Booking System

If you'd like people to book appointments or calls through your website, then you'll need a calendar booking system. Again, if you've chosen a platform to create your website that includes this, then you're sorted. But if not, we recommend Calendly.com. It links well with any website platform and also to online meeting/conferencing platforms if you're booking online calls or meetings.

Online Video Meeting/Conferencing Platform

There are a few options out there, but Zoom.com is our go to for simple calls and webinars. Most people are familiar with it, especially after it became people's go to for communicating with family for a couple of years, and because it's popular, it integrates well with other systems. It also connects up to Facebook to run training or webinars in Facebook groups.

Google Analytics

We talk about the benefits of using analytics later in the book. Some website platforms have their own analytics, but where you are able to use an external tool we recommend linking up Google Analytics. It's free and provides so much data that is beneficial to you improving your business marketing and targeting.

Payment Gateways

If you are taking payments through your website, you'll need to have a payment gateway that collects the money, whatever website platform you use. We personally prefer Stripe.com for this and use it for all of our products and services. We find the reporting and tracking fairly simple, and you have a lot of control over when you want your money paid out to you.

PayPal.com is another good option, especially for lower priced products or services because people can pay for them from their PayPal credit and don't even have to go and find their card details. It takes away a possible objection they could have to buying if you make it as easy as possible. We only have PayPal as a payment option for our low price products because we don't find the reporting as easy.

As with everything else, have a look and see which one you think will work best for you.

Making the Decision

We are going to be honest with you. Even with your website shopping list and the information in this book, you will have to invest a bit of time in making the decision about the platform and the supporting tech you choose. There will be some that you can easily eliminate if they don't do some things you need or if the price really is out of reach for you at the moment, but others won't be that easy to make a decision on.

Whenever you can, we recommend you actually test out the platform or tech. Many of them offer a free trial for a month, so you can go in and have a play, look at their "how to" materials and possibly even submit a question to their support team to see how responsive and helpful they are.

Those who don't give you a trial may offer demos, so have one of those. If you're worried about doing that because you think it will turn into a sales call, let them know when you book or conversationally near the start of the call, that you are in the research stage and you are still considering a few options. Do the same if you're considering the bespoke route and are talking to developers. Anyone who really understands this industry won't push for a sale if it's not a good fit because they know that's not beneficial to either party.

CHAPTER 4
WEB DESIGN HINTS AND TIPS

WHY GOOD DESIGN MATTERS

When you're creating your website, the way it looks is really important. A good design will create a feeling of professionalism, and, as we mentioned earlier in the book, one of the things your website should do is be professional. You're running a professional business and so your website needs to reflect that.

Design also matters because doing it well means your website visitors will have a nice experience using your website. They'll be able to find what they're looking for easily, making them much more likely to take action. When people have a positive experience, they can be sold to more easily. If they have a negative experience, their reaction will be to walk away.

Good design can also actually guide your website visitor into doing what you want them to do, so your website achieves its purpose and so you can help them in the best way possible. Here are six tips around design which you can use on your website to ensure you have happy website visitors.

1. GIVE THINGS ROOM TO BREATHE

It's a very good idea to leave a generous amount of space around each section on a web page. Designers will refer to this as "white space" even if the background colour isn't white.

If you take a look at the web page below, which is the Work with Me page taken from our Coach website template, it isn't cluttered so your eye can easily move around and find what you're looking for. Too much clutter can annoy a website visitor or confuse them, and unless you are the only person who runs a business like yours, they'll leave your website and look elsewhere.

Example of using "white space"

2. VISUAL HIERARCHY

You need to give your web pages consistent visual hierarchy. Visual hierarchy is where the main heading on the page is in the largest font and from there, the font size decreases with the decreasing importance of the content. Often the headings will get smaller as you move down the page, but if you have a section that has equal importance as another heading, then those headings should be the same size.

Having consistent visual hierarchy makes it easier for your website visitor to see the key messages you're trying to get across and focus on the parts of your website that are important to them.

The home page of the Fitness website template below shows a clear visual hierarchy and a key tip to keep in mind is that you should only have one H1 heading (the biggest one) on each page. This is best practice for that all important Search Engine Optimisation (SEO).

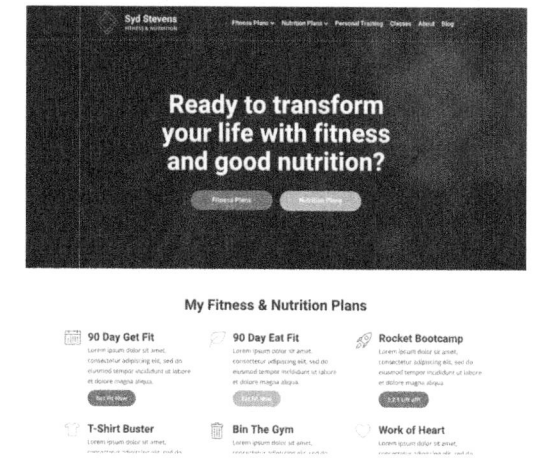

Example of visual hierarchy

3. IMAGES ARE EVERYTHING

We cover this in the planning section, but it's so key we want to reiterate it. We often hear ourselves uttering the words, "images make or break a website", and it's true! You can have the most beautifully laid out website, with the most engaging copy, but if your images look dull, unprofessional and unengaging then your website visitor might not even get to looking around your site and reading your copy. People make very quick, snap decisions these days, so you need to do everything you can to encourage them to make the decision to stay and look around.

In the example below, if the images of food were dull and unappetising, you wouldn't want to find out about Anna's nutrition tips, but the bright, vibrant, delicious looking food in the photos make you want to take a look.

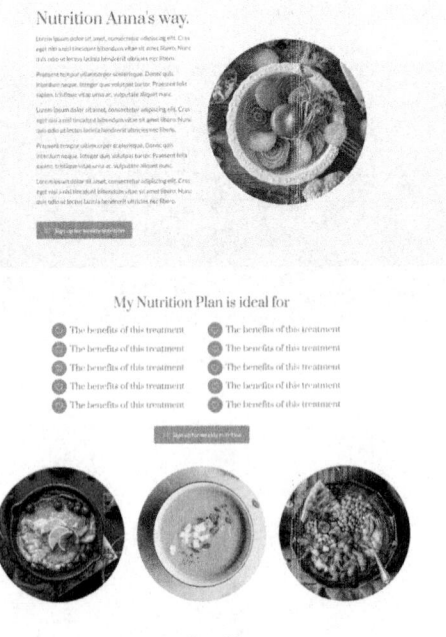

Example of good imagery

4. GETTING TYPOGRAPHY RIGHT

We have already mentioned visual hierarchy, but you need to consider your font choices as well. Don't go crazy with fonts. Only pick two: one for headings and one for the content. If you use more than two, everything starts looking busy again and it's hard for your potential customers to focus and find what they're looking for. There may be the odd occasion where you can add a third font in to add a little flourish or extra emphasis to a word. You can see an example of this with the script font used for the word "unlock" on the Wellness website template below. But use this third font sparingly!

Example of good typography with a flourish font

Choose two fonts that pair well together. To do this you can try a few combinations next to each other or use a tool like Google Fonts. In that tool, once you've chosen a first font, it will suggest other fonts that go well with it.

Also consider how you want to be portrayed. In the Wellness website template, a script front and serif font are used which both flow nicely and add a sense of calm.

In contrast, in the Speaker website template, a bold, sans-serif font is used that conveys a strong personality.

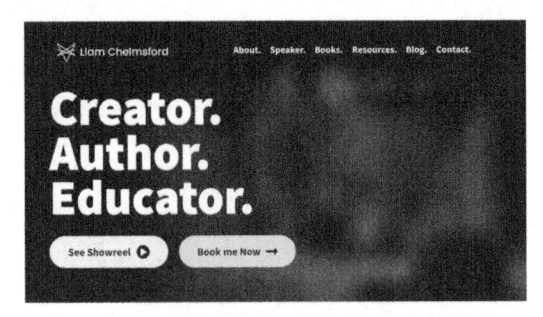

Example of bold typography

A quick overview of fonts

There a number of classifications of typeface.

Serif Typeface

Serif typefaces have the little decorative flicks and extensions at the end of some strokes; these are called "serifs", hence the name. The most well known serif typeface is probably:

Times New Roman

Serif typeface example

Sans-Serif Typeface

Sans-serif literally translates to without-serif, so it doesn't have the flicks and extensions. A popular sans-serif typeface is:

Arial

Sans-serif typeface example

Slab Serif

This is much like serif but heavier. An example of a slab serif font is:

Patua One

Slab Serif typeface example

Script and Cursive

Script and cursive usually emulate handwriting. An example of this is:

Caveat

Script typeface example

Just be careful when you are choosing a font, especially a script font, and consider the words you will want to have in that font. Why? Because the flourishes and spacing can make it difficult to read some words, so test the font well before you use it. Also, there have been instances where words look like other, sometimes rude, words which could be embarrassing!

5. MAKE CALLS TO ACTION STAND OUT

Most of the time your calls to action will be buttons on your website, such as a button that says, "Buy Now" or "Book a Call". But sometimes they will be links within your content. Whatever form they take, they need to stand out, be consistent and be clear.

If you have had your brand created for you, your brand designer will have given you a colour palette and within that they will have identified accent colours for you to use. It is often these accent colours that you would use for your call to action buttons or links. They are colours that will stand out and draw your website visitor's eye to them.

Don't use this colour for any text other than your link text, otherwise your website visitor will get confused and frustrated if they are trying to click on something that isn't clickable. Remember, annoying your website visitor is one sure fire way of losing them and sending them off to one of your competitors.

On the main pages of your website, you should try to have two call to action buttons:

1. one to reflect the main purpose of your website, this call to action should stand out the most, and
2. the other to reflect the secondary purpose of your website.

In the following example of the Ready Steady Websites® home page, you can see the "Join Now" button stands out in the bright green colour and the "Free Resources" button is also clear in the grey but isn't as eye catching so doesn't detract from the primary purpose.

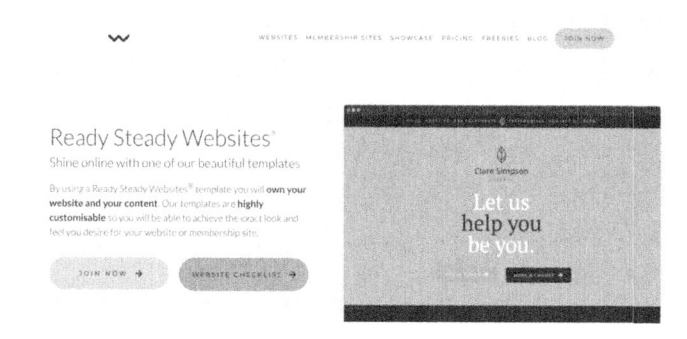

6. TEST, TEST AND TEST AGAIN

Once your website is looking good, you've connected up all the tech, and you're happy with the content, you may think it's time to send it live and shout about it to the entire world – but you are wrong. But you already know that because you've seen the title above this paragraph, so you know that you need to test your website first.

We've repeated the word "test" three times because you need to test your website on a computer, on a tablet and on a mobile. Then if you make any tweaks as you go on one of the screen sizes, you need to go back and check it still looks and works OK on the others, which is where the "again" bit comes in.

We talked earlier in the book about why it's important your website works on all devices and about how quickly people make decisions these days about a company based on their website: it really does need to work well and look good.

Here is a checklist to follow of everything you should test on each size of device, and like we said, if you make a change, go back and check how it looks and works on the other sizes again to make sure they haven't been affected.

Website Testing Checklist

- Click on every main menu item.
- Click on every footer menu item.

For each page:

- Scroll down the whole page looking at the overall look and feel of the page; check that spacing and text sizes are consistent and images appear properly.
- Click on every link and button.
- Sign up for any resources or calls that are available for free to check the process works.
- Check you have received all the emails you should as a website owner when someone has signed up.
- Check you have received all the emails the person who has signed up should.
- If you have products or services to buy, actually buy one, paying on a real card, not a test account.
- Check you have received all the emails and notifications you should as a website owner when someone buys.
- Check you have received all the emails and products the person who buys should.
- Now refund yourself for the purchase.
- Check you have received all the emails and notifications you should as a website owner when someone requests a refund.
- Check you have received all the emails the person who requests a refund should.

Key things to check on smaller screen sizes:

- That images and headings don't vanish off the side of the screen.
- That pop ups don't overfill the screen so you can't get out of them.

CHAPTER 5
EVERYTHING AFTER YOUR WEBSITE IS LIVE: CONTENT, MAINTENANCE AND TRAFFIC

THE IMPORTANCE OF ADDING NEW CONTENT REGULARLY

So, your website is planned, you've identified the method you're going to use to create it, and once it's created you may think it's time to relax, put your feet up and admire your finished website like it's a painting on the wall. Well, you've worked hard so we will let you do that for a couple of days, but then that's it!!

A website isn't a painting. It needs adding to and tweaking regularly for it to perform to its full potential. There are a couple of key reasons for making sure you update and add new content to your website regularly.

The first is that when someone comes to your website, they are unlikely to buy from you straight away. They will be doing their research, checking you out and comparing you to others in your industry. When they come back to your website again and see that a new blog post has been added or there's a new testimonial on your home page, then they're going to be impressed. They're going to see that you are currently working with clients and that you're active in sharing your knowledge through your blog.

The second is that search engines favour websites that have new content added regularly. When new content is added, the search engine bots come along and reindex your website. So basically by adding new content, you're reminding Google and its counterparts that you are there, which can only be a good thing.

An added bonus is that by adding new content to your website, you're also giving yourself content to share elsewhere, maybe to social media or in your email newsletter, making those jobs easier for you. This has another added bonus, the more traffic you send to your website through links on social media and your email newsletters, and just by mentioning it on networking calls or in meetings, the better this is for your SEO.

So, by looking at all of this, you can see why you shouldn't just leave your website sitting there.

As well as adding new content such as blogs, testimonials, case studies or portfolio items, you should also keep an eye on your main website page content. Check that nothing has gone out of date on a regular basis. What kinds of things are we talking about? These:

- the number of years you have been in business (although you can get around this by saying when you launched),
- your team members, and
- your photos – make sure they haven't got so old that you're no longer recognisable in them!

We recommend you put a reminder in your calendar every three months to do a quick check that everything is still accurate and the language you're using still reflects you and your business.

REGULAR ONGOING CONTENT PLANNING

To help you stay on track with creating regular content for your website and to keep driving traffic to it, we have created these planning sheets. You can download them as printable worksheets here: https://readysteadywebsites.com/handbook-resources/, and we have also recorded a little tutorial to talk you through how to best use them which you can get through the link above.

Select the types of content you will use on your website (circle up to three):

Blog Posts	Podcast	Vlogs
Case Studies	Testimonials	Gallery Images
Portfolio	Other:	

Commit to how often you will post to your website:

Content Type	Frequency (circle)		
	Weekly	Bi-weekly	Monthly
	Weekly	Bi-weekly	Monthly
	Weekly	Bi-weekly	Monthly

Commit to the day or date you will post to your website:

Content type	Day of the week/date of the month

Now you have your content planned, take time to block out time in your calendar for creating and posting this content. You may wish to batch create it every quarter or month, or you could set time aside each week. Whatever works best for you. Tick off when you have it booked in here.

☐ Done

Vlog/Podcast/Blog Ideas

Here are some ideas to get you started with your long form content, whether you do it in written, audio or video format. We have also left some space for you to write your own. You can tick them off when you have used them.

Some Topic Ideas for You	✔	Your Topic Ideas	✔
01 Write about a common problem or problems that a lot of your ideal clients would have and give them the solution.			
02 Write about your business journey and how your experience has helped you serve your clients better.			
03 Write about how investing in your service or product is important, how it will benefit your ideal client.			
04 Write about a common problem or problems that a lot of your ideal clients would have and then tell them about a free resource or one of your services that would help them and link to it.			
05 Write a "Top 5" post around your area of business or expertise.			
06 Write an in-depth case study about the work you have done with one of your clients or the experience one of your customers has had with your product.			
07 Write a post around some research carried out in your industry.			
08 Write a post about a milestone in your business and thank the people who got you there, including your clients.			
09 Write a personal profile.			
10 Write a "How To" post.			
11 Write a post about why you love what you do.			
12 Write about a collaboration you are part of.			

Try to include a call to action towards the end of each of your blog posts. Sometimes this may be to read one of your other blog posts that is relevant; sometimes this will be to one of your freebies, which will mean you are building your mailing list; and sometimes you could get them to take a look at one of your paid for services or products.

Guest Blogging Ideas

Guest blogging is great, both to host guest bloggers to get a range of content on your website but also to guest on other people's websites to get in front of a new audience and have a link back to your website.

Have a think about topics your audience would benefit from learning about that would fit well on a blog on your website. Make a list of the topics and make a note of who you could approach to write about them. You can tick it off once you've got them booked in.

Guest Topic Ideas	Potential Guest Blogger	✓

Email List Building and Newsletter Content Planning

Using your website to build your email list is a great way of capturing leads, and we want to help you plan how you'll do this. First, choose up to three types of lead magnet that you would like to use to build your email list:

Free Download	Blog Subscription	Quiz
Plan/Service Picker	Free Workshop	Mini Course
eBook	Other:	

Set the date you'll have each lead magnet created by. You don't have to do them all at once. In fact it's better to focus on creating and launching one and seeing how that goes, and then launching others later.

Lead Magnet Type	Launch Date

Now you've identified the lead magnets you're going to use, put the launch date in your calendar and also block out time in your calendar for creating the lead magnet and the landing page for it.

Once you've created your lead magnet, it's important to nurture the relationship with the people who sign up, so make sure you plan and create a few emails to go out once they've received the download or the answer to their quiz etc. In these automated emails it works well to include a call to action, such as letting them know they can follow you on social media, telling them about another resource they would find useful or asking them questions and asking them to reply to your email with their answer. You could also offer them something to buy, but it should be a low price item at this stage.

Too many automated emails feel impersonal, so a follow up of three or four emails works quite well, and you should also add your new subscriber to your regular email newsletter (we'll look at that more later in this section).

You can start planning your automated emails here:

Email 1 – Sent when they receive what they sign up for.

Main message you want to convey in this email:
Call to action:

Email 2 – Sent ...... days after email 1

Main message you want to convey in this email:
Call to action:

Email 3 – Sent ...... days after email 2

Main message you want to convey in this email:
Call to action:

Email 4 – Sent ...... days after email 3

Main message you want to convey in this email:
Call to action:

Now plan in some time in your calendar to write these emails and add them into your email automation sequence in your email system. Tick when you've booked it in here:

☐ Done

Now you're getting people joining your email list, you need to think about your email newsletter.

Select how often you'll commit to sending out an email newsletter (circle one):

Weekly	Bi-weekly	Monthly

Here are some newsletter content ideas. Select what you'll include in your newsletter. You need to include enough that people want to stay on your list and are interested to see what's included each time they receive it but don't make it so long that it's a drag to get through because people will stop engaging with it.

Some of your content choices will be determined by the content you have planned to include on your website.

Circle the content you will include in your newsletter:

Intro and link to blog	Intro and link to vlog	Intro and link to podcast	Highlight new case study and link to it
Highlight new portfolio item and link to it	Include a new testimonial and thank the client	Link to free resource	Link to useful content on someone else's website
"How to work with me" section	Tip of the week/month	Social media links	Other:

HOW TO DRIVE TRAFFIC TO YOUR WEBSITE (USING ANALYTICS)

It's important to send traffic to your website regularly. Some of the ways of doing this that we have already mentioned are to link to it from your email newsletters and to get guest blogging opportunities. There are many other ways to drive traffic to your website. We recommend you focus on three that you'll do regularly but when new opportunities come up, grab them whenever you can. The more traffic you're sending to your website from a range of sources, the better.

If your website is more established, a really good way of deciding where to focus your energy to drive traffic to your site is to look at your analytics. We use Google Analytics, but some website platforms have their own analytics. We recommend you review your analytics on a monthly basis to see where the traffic is coming from that hits your website. You can see which social media platforms are sending traffic to your website, which other websites are sending traffic to your website and the search terms that people are using that make them end up on your website. This last one is really useful in helping you decide on the things you could be writing blog posts or recording podcasts about.

If you're spending loads of time on Facebook but your analytics shows there isn't much traffic coming from there but even with just a little bit of time on Pinterest you are getting much more traffic from there, then you know it's worth focusing more time on putting content on Pinterest.

If your website isn't established, then it's worth picking the methods and platforms you feel most comfortable with to send traffic to your website and keeping an eye on your analytics. If you can see some of these are working then stick with them, but if others aren't try something else.

It takes time and consistent work to get good SEO results, but if you put the work in on the right things, it will pay off in the end. Also don't think that everything has to be done through social media and links from other websites. Building actual relationships with people is key too, whether this is through networking activities or being friendly and chatty with people in your day to day interactions with them.

Some of our best converting website traffic comes from being featured on websites or recommended by people because we took the time to get to know them and support them.

Taking all of this into consideration, choose the methods you will use frequently to signpost people to your website:

Facebook	LinkedIn	Pinterest	Instagram Post (Link in bio)
Instagram Stories (Direct Link)	Email Newsletter	Networking	Guest Blogging
Guest Podcast Interviews	Sponsorship Opportunities	YouTube	Other:

Now you know where you're going to share your website think about how frequently you'll commit to doing so.

Sharing Method	Sharing Frequency			
	Twice a week	Weekly	Bi-weekly	Monthly
	Twice a week	Weekly	Bi-weekly	Monthly
	Twice a week	Weekly	Bi-weekly	Monthly

Now in your calendar or planner book in the days you'll share your website by these methods. Tick when you've booked it in here:

☐ Done

Social Media Post Planning to Share Your Website

It's all well and good deciding on the social media platform you're going to post to and how often you'll do it, but the tricky bit is actually working out what to post. Just like putting new content on your website, consistency is key when it comes to posting on social media. Now, we aren't social media experts, but we do have some tips for the kinds of posts you can use that will share your website content. Remember, though, every time you post on social media shouldn't be purely to drive people to your website – you need to mix it in with entertaining posts, posts that ask questions to get engagement, sharing other people's posts if they're useful to your audience and some top tips that show off your knowledge but also really help people.

In this section, you'll find some social media post suggestions that will drive traffic to your website. Choose the ones that you feel most comfortable creating and sharing because then you'll be more likely to actually do it. Once you've identified the types of post you're going to use, put them down in your calendar or planner next to the days you have allocated to share your website on social media so you're committing to yourself that you will do it! You'll probably think of lots more as you get used to sharing your website on social media, but these will get you started.

If you are using Instagram, we recommend setting up a links page on your website. Don't use something like Linktree. You want all the traffic to be going directly to your website. Make sure you keep this page up to date. That said, don't worry about changing the link to your most recent post/vlog/podcast episode, just have a link to the main page for those on there. Then when you direct people to your latest post or episode from your Instagram post say something like, "Follow the link in my bio to my blog". If you are releasing weekly posts, you're making more work for yourself trying to change your links page every week. Also, if you forget one week, you'll be losing website visitors who were interested in that post when they got to your links page and found it's not there.

Though you do need to keep an eye on your links page regularly and make sure you have the most relevant links at the top. Remember to also remove ones that are no longer relevant. Otherwise it's going to get too cluttered, and we've already talked about why that's a bad thing.

With Facebook and LinkedIn, it's a good idea to have some posts where you don't put the link in the actual post but make it more of a conversational post and then drop the link in the comments "in case anyone would like to see more". This is a tip we have picked up from a few people who support businesses with their social media because posts without external links are more likely to be shown to more people apparently.

With every social media platform, it's important that you don't just post, but go and comment on other people's posts as well. Why? Because when people see you commenting on things, they're more likely to go and check out your posts.

Facebook and Instagram suggestions:

- A simple post with a short intro and featured image linking to a new post/vlog/podcast episode, then turn this post into a story on Facebook or Instagram. Then you have two pieces of content in one!
- Create a short video or reel discussing a top tip from a new post/vlog/podcast episode and link to it. Turn this video or reel into a story on Facebook or Instagram, too.
- A "Top Tips" graphic in a post linking to a relevant post/vlog/podcast episode. You know what we're going to say, you can also turn this into a story on Facebook or Instagram.
- An interactive question in a Facebook or Instagram story such as "Are You Using Testimonials on Your Website?" with yes and no buttons to click, then a link to a relevant

post/vlog/podcast episode about why they should be.
- A nice graphic of a quote from a new testimonial and a link to other testimonials on your website or to a case study of that work. Again, turn it into a story.
- An image carousel of new work that you've added to your portfolio with a link to see more. Also, create a story using one of the images.
- Share beautiful images of your products or services in action alongside a testimonial.

Facebook group suggestions:

The way we find Facebook most powerful is to get involved in relevant Facebook groups. Answer questions, get known and look out for posts asking for what you do.

If there are any threads where you can share your business, do that. If you're in a group that allows you to promote, do put a promo post in every now and then – but put in more posts that aren't sales based. These groups are often great for finding guest bloggers, which shows you are willing to support other people. When you do that, they're more likely to recommend you.

There are also a few things you really shouldn't do. Don't get salesy when you respond to posts asking for what you do. Instead, just let them know you offer what they need, offer to have a chat if they would like to and pop in the link to your website. We suggest you don't DM them unless they have asked you to.

LinkedIn suggestions:

- Create a poll that leads nicely into a discussion about your latest post/vlog/podcast episode and

then share the link in the comments once the discussion has got started.
- Create an image carousel of new work that you have added to your portfolio with a link to see more.
- Create a simple post with a short intro and featured image linking to a new post/vlog/podcast episode.
- Go live and share some advice or top tips and tell your connections about your recent post/vlog/podcast episode that they might find useful.
- A nice graphic of a quote from a new testimonial and a link to other testimonials on your website or to a case study of that work and turn it into a post or article.
- Share beautiful images of your products or services in action alongside a testimonial.

Pinterest suggestions:

- Create a couple of different visual pins for each post/vlog/podcast episode.
- Create a video pin about a post/vlog/podcast episode. Make sure you choose a section or post/episode that lends itself to being talked about on video.
- Create image pins for new testimonials you have received.
- Create image pins for products using lovely product photography.

MAINTAINING YOUR WEBSITE

So, now you have your website, you're adding your blog posts and testimonials to it regularly, and you're sending a nice flow of traffic to it. You need to make sure you are maintaining it. Below, you'll find the four things we suggest you keep an eye on.

1. General content is up to date

It doesn't give a good impression to your website visitor if content is out of date on your website. They may even wonder whether you're actually still in business, so make sure you are checking up on this monthly or quarterly, depending on how often things change in your business.

2. Images are recent

As we've already mentioned, ensuring your branding is consistent with every check point is key. If you are the face of your business, people know what you look like from networking or social media. If they then come to your website and see a photo of you from 10 or 20 years ago, that's going to be a bit of a jarring experience. People won't expect that and that feeling will reduce your authenticity and move them a step away from buying. You and your website will then have to work harder to bring them back.

3. Page loading speed is good

Making sure your website loads quickly is really important. Firstly, because if your website takes ages to load, your website visitors might not hang around to wait for it to appear and will go elsewhere. Secondly, because the faster your website loads, the more Google will like it, so it's important for SEO too.

You'll be able to check this yourself by visiting your website and finding out whether it seems to be loading OK. But you can also use an online tool called GTmetrix.com.

You type your web address into GT Metrix and get a score for how well it's performing for page loading speed. If you score a C or higher, it's OK, but you want to be aiming for an A. If your website isn't performing well, it's often to do with image sizes, but GT Metrix will give you a list of things that need improving on your website to help you increase your page loading speed.

4. Links are still working

We recommend you check if your website has any broken links every quarter. This can happen quite easily if you have linked to an external website from a blog post and that has been removed or even if you yourself have removed a page from your website and forgotten that you had linked to it from somewhere else on the website.

A tool you can use to help you with this is ahrefs.com/broken-link-checker. It really is worth keeping on top of this regularly otherwise it can become a big task. You can schedule ahrefs to check your site regularly, and then you'll receive an email letting you know if you have broken links which will help keep you on track with this!

CHAPTER 6
CONCLUSION

HOW TO MAKE SURE YOU ACTUALLY DO EVERYTHING WE'VE COVERED

So, we've gone through each stage of planning and creating your website, but we know the reality of seeing how the whole process works is very different to actually doing it. We want to make sure you actually take action and create and maintain and fantastic website that is an asset to your business.

Some top tips

Set yourself website-related goals each week. For each goal, set date that you will have achieved this by.

Block out time in your diary to do this and make that non-negotiable. This reminds us of the story of the coach who cancelled "website time" for client calls. By doing that she was essentially putting off making her first sale and gaining her first client through her website.

Keep yourself accountable. The best way of doing this is telling somebody what you're planning on achieving and by when. Then you'll feel much more inclined to do it because you won't want to look silly. Also, consider the money you've invested in buying this book and the amount of time it has taken to read. That is a massive waste of your time if you don't actually put what you've learnt into action. Use that thought to push you forward.

Don't procrastinate. We heard a brilliant tip from Trudy Simmons, a clarity and productivity coach, if you know there are certain tasks you use to procrastinate with, block time out to do those at the start of each day, then they aren't there to distract you anymore and you can get on with creating or updating your website!

If you still know that you're going to struggle to stay on track with creating or maintaining your website, we run our Ready Steady Websites® Mentoring Membership to help you stay on track and to provide ongoing advice and support.

We aren't the only people who offer this kind of thing. There are lots of accountability, mentoring and coaching services out there that will ensure you meet your goals. So, if you know you need that support to make you take action, then please find the right person to support you.

FINAL THOUGHTS

By creating an amazing website, you can reach more people who can benefit from your services. That means you can help more people, which should be at the core of any business.

Some people feel they don't want to shout about their business too much. If you feel like that, think about some of the best testimonials you've ever received. The ones where people are so happy with the service they've received from you, the ones where they're gushing about how much difference you have made to them, the ones where they can't recommend you enough. If they had never heard of you, you wouldn't have been able to have an impact on that person's life, and their life would have been worse for it.

So, you owe it to your future clients to take your website seriously, do the planning and the work that's needed so you can generate leads and make sales – that's what will allow you to help as many people as possible!

WORK WITH US

READY STEADY WEBSITES® TEMPLATES

Shine online with one of our beautiful templates.
By using a Ready Steady Websites® template you will own your website and your content. Our templates are highly customisable so you will be able to achieve the exact look and feel you desire for your website or membership site.

www.readysteadywebsites.com

READY STEADY WEBSITES® MENTORING MEMBERSHIP

A membership focused all around websites. The Mentoring Membership will give you the support and confidence to create an amazing website that genuinely helps your business to thrive.

Whatever stage you are at with your website and whatever platform you are on, we can guide and support you to grow in confidence with structuring your website, adding new content and sending traffic to it. We will also keep you accountable so that you actually get it done and share it with pride so that it can start generating leads and making sales.

readysteadywebsites.com/mm/

ABOUT THE AUTHORS

Jude and Chris Wharton are a husband and wife team and the co-founders of Ready Steady Websites®, an off the shelf website and membership site template service. They launched Ready Steady Websites® in 2019 and they have been running a successful digital design company, 2nd Floor Designs Ltd since 2010.

Chris' professional experience started in the early 2000s in web and digital. He's successfully managed, consulted and worked on projects for RBS, Renault, Coutts Bank, IKEA, Mazda, Kia, WorldPay, Olympus, Grant Thornton, RAC and Masterclass, as well as some lesser known but equally as amazing international and local brands and businesses.

Chris has a wide range of skills including digital consultancy, UI design, UX and web build, sketch and illustration and project management.

Jude has a background in youth work, education and training as well as people and project management and has delivered workshops in Westminster. She has a CMI Level 5 Award in Management and Leadership and a BA (Hons) degree in Education and Training. All of this experience she brings to managing the business and creating learning materials for Ready Steady Websites®.

facebook.com/readysteadywebsites
instagram.com/readysteadywebsites

ACKNOWLEDGMENTS

Ooh, it's our Oscars moment! Don't play the music just yet.

Firstly, we would like to thank everyone who has supported us in our business over the last 12 years. Thank you to everyone who saw the potential in our Ready Steady Websites® idea who has used the service, recommended it, invited us to be on their podcasts or to deliver training to their audience, feature on their blog or in their magazine etc. There are so many of you and for that we are really grateful.

Thank you in particular to some of our business friends who have consistently supported us and cheered us on over the years or gone the extra mile in getting us in front of the right people – Maria, Gwen, Toni, Stu, Jacqui, Kate, Trudy, Emily and Alan, Mossy, Sophie, David, Michael, Shari, Catherine and we know there are more but they will start playing the music.

Thank you to the friends we have who don't run their own business but who get it. When we speak to others in business, we realise you are like unicorns and we really appreciate you.

Thank you to Carrie Green and the FEA for running your Create and Sell programme that gave us the guidance and accountability we needed to get this book written and out there and thank you to everyone who supported us through that programme especially Katie a fab mentor and Nicole and Freddy who were fantastic accountability buddies!

Thank you to Jennifer Jones for not only being a brilliant

editor but also for telling everyone how amazing this book is and how glad she was to have read it.

Also, thank you to our parents without whom we wouldn't be here. (That's an acknowledgments requirement but it doesn't mean we don't mean it!) Thank you to our two wonderful boys for putting up with us whilst we juggled family life and business to get this book finished.

And thank you to you for reading literally to the end of the book!

You can play the music now.

BIBLIOGRAPHY

1. INTRODUCTION

1. https://www.smartinsights.com/mobile-marketing/mobile-marketing-analytics/mobile-marketing-statistics/
2. https://www.campaignmonitor.com/resources/infographics/email-marketing-vs-other-digital-marketing-channels/

2. THE WEBSITE PLANNING PROCESS

1. https://buildingastorybrand.com/

3. CHOOSING YOUR PLATFORM AND SUPPORTING TECH

1. https://kinsta.com/blog/wordpress-statistics/

Printed in Great Britain
by Amazon